BIBLE ACTIVITIES FOR KIDS

Vickie Save

Illustrated by Ken Save

BARBOUR BOOKS
An Imprint of Barbour Publishing, Inc.

Published by Barbour Books, an imprint of Barbour Publishing, Inc., P.O. Box 719, Uhrichsville, Ohio 44683, www.barbourbooks.com

Member of the
Evangelical Christian
Publishers Association

Printed in the United States of America.
5 4 3

BIBLE ACTIVITIES FOR KIDS

COLOR *the* PICTURE

The Book of ROMANS

PAUL WROTE THE BOOK OF ROMANS FOR THE CHRISTIANS LIVING IN ROME.

THE PURPOSE FOR THIS LETTER WAS TO TEACH THAT NONE ARE PERFECT OR ABLE TO IMPRESS GOD. THERE IS ONLY ONE WHO IS PERFECT AND THAT IS JESUS CHRIST.

WHEN WE PUT OUR TRUST AND FAITH IN THE PERSON OF JESUS CHRIST, WE ARE FREE FROM THE POWER OF SIN. THROUGH JESUS' DEATH ON THE CROSS THE SIN ISSUE HAS BEEN SETTLED ONCE AND FOR ALL. THROUGH THE RESURRECTED LIFE OF CHRIST LIVING IN US, WE ARE GIVEN A NEW LIFE. WE ARE TOTALLY ACCEPTED AND LOVED BY GOD—NOT BY OUR OWN WORKS BUT BY THE WORK OF GOD'S SON, JESUS CHRIST.

DOUBLE *the* FUN

UNSCRAMBLE THE UNDERLINED WORDS IN EACH VERSE. ON THE NEXT PAGE, PLACE YOUR ANSWERS IN THE SPACES PROVIDED AND THEN COMPLETE THE CROSSWORD PUZZLE.

1. "PAUL, A SERVANT OF JESUS CHRIST, CALLED TO BE AN APOSTLE, SEPARATED UNTO THE <u>LGEOPS</u> OF GOD, (WHICH HE HAD PROMISED AFORE BY HIS <u>STRPEOHP</u> IN THE HOLY SCRIPTURES,) CONCERNING HIS SON JESUS CHRIST OUR LORD, WHICH WAS MADE OF THE SEED OF DAVID ACCORDING TO THE FLESH."

ROMANS 1:1–3, KJV

2. "AND DECLARED TO BE THE SON OF GOD WITH <u>RPEWO</u>, ACCORDING TO THE <u>TSIPIR</u> OF HOLINESS, BY THE RESURRECTION FROM THE DEAD."

ROMANS 1:4, KJV

3. "<u>EGCRA</u> TO YOU AND PEACE FROM GOD OUR <u>RFEAHT</u>, AND THE LORD JESUS <u>TCHSIR</u>."

ROMANS 1:7, KJV

1. _____ _____

2. _____ _____

3. _____ _____

   _____

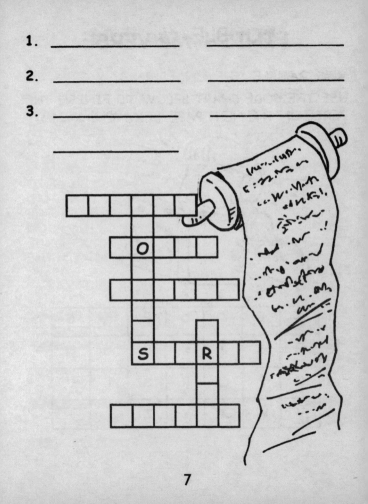

FINISH *the* VERSE

USE THE CODE CHART BELOW TO FINISH THE
VERSE ON THE NEXT PAGE. (EXAMPLE: K=24)

	1	2	3	4	5	6	7
1	A	B	C	D	E	F	G
2	H	I	J	K	L	M	N
3	O	P	Q	R	S	T	U
4	V	W	X	Y	Z		

"I AM NOT <u>a s h a m e d</u>
<small>11 35 21 11 26 15 14</small>

OF   THE   <u>g o s p e l</u>,
<small>17 31 35 32 15 25</small>

BECAUSE   IT   IS   THE

<u>p o w e r</u> OF <u>G o d</u> FOR
<small>32 31 42 15 34   17 31 14</small>

THE   <u>s a l v a t i o n</u>
<small>35 11 25 41 11 36 22 31 27</small>

OF <u>e v e r y o n e</u> WHO
<small>15 41 15 34 44 31 27 15</small>

BELIEVES: FIRST FOR THE <u>j e w</u>
<small>23 15 42</small>

THEN FOR THE <u>g e n t i l e</u>."
<small>17 15 27 36 22 25 15</small>

ROMANS 1:16

9

SCRAMBLED VERSES

UNSCRAMBLE THE WORDS BELOW AND
COMPLETE THE VERSE ON THE NEXT PAGE.

"EHT HWART FO DGO SI GIBEN
ERLVAEDE MFOR NHEEVA GAAISTN
LAL EHT DGOSLESNSES DNA
SWCIKDEENS FO NME OHW SPUSSERP
EHT THTUR YB RTIHE SWCIKDEENS,
ECNIS THWA YMA EB NKWNO TBAUO
DGO SI NLPIA OT MTEH, EBACUSE
DGO SHA EMDA TI NLPIA OT MTEH."

"The _____ ___
___ ___ _____
___ ___ ___ ___ ___
___ ___ ___ ___ ___
___ ___ ___ ___ ___-
___ ___ ___ ___ ___-
___ ___ ___ ___ ___
___ ___ ___ ___ ___
___ ___ ___ ___ ___
___ ___ ___ ___ ___-
_____, _____ ____
___ ___ ___ ___ ___
___ ___ ___ ___ ___
_____ ___ _____,
___ ___ ___ ___
___ ___ ___." ___
___ _____."

ROMANS 1:18–19

WORD SEARCH

FIND THE WORDS LISTED BELOW IN THE
WORD SEARCH ON THE NEXT PAGE.

GRACE   PEACE   FATHER

POWER

WORKS   GENTILE

CHRIST

PERFECT   JEW

PROPHETS   SPIRIT

```
H R Q L F A T H E R F D
F J G O N C L M F K C W
G S J V P O W E R A A B
R D S E B D F E R R K L
A N P P E L W G G O R R
C P I R B W O R K S O D
E Z R E B V C X U R S T
W A I T R B C H R I S T
H A T P I N T M E J E W
Q L R V B C T S S D C L
M W I B E P D P E A C E
B Y D F B C E K C H L Q
T C R P A G E N T I L E
N E J E B G E N T E N W
P R O P H E T S Q I O P
```

FILL *in the* BLANKS

USING THE WORDS BELOW, COMPLETE THE
VERSE ON THE NEXT PAGE.

CREATION   WORLD
INVISIBLE   ETERNAL
MEN   DIVINE
CLEARLY   UNDERSTOOD
MADE   EXCUSE

"FOR SINCE THE _____ OF
THE _____ GOD'S
_____ QUALITIES—
HIS _____ POWER AND
_____ NATURE — HAVE
BEEN _____ SEEN, BEING
_____ FROM WHAT
HAS BEEN _____, SO THAT
_____ ARE WITHOUT
_____."

ROMANS 1:20

15

CROSSWORD

ACROSS

1. "FOR ALTHOUGH THEY KNEW _____."
2. "THEY NEITHER _____ HIM AS GOD NOR GAVE THANKS TO HIM."
3. "BUT THEIR THINKING BECAME _____."
4. "AND THEIR FOOLISH _____ WERE DARKENED."

DOWN

1. "ALTHOUGH THEY _____ TO BE WISE."
2. "THEY _____ FOOLS."
3. "AND EXCHANGED THE _____ OF THE IMMORTAL GOD."
4. "FOR IMAGES MADE TO LOOK LIKE MORTAL MAN AND BIRDS AND _____ AND REPTILES."

COLOR *the* PICTURE

"FOR THEREIN IS THE RIGHTEOUSNESS OF GOD REVEALED FROM FAITH TO FAITH: AS IT IS WRITTEN, THE JUST SHALL LIVE BY FAITH."

ROMANS 1:17, KJV

SCRAMBLED VERSES

UNSCRAMBLE THE WORDS BELOW AND COMPLETE THE VERSE ON THE NEXT PAGE.

"UYO, TEHROEFRE, EHVA ON XESCEU, UYO WOH SPSA TJNUEDMG NO ESNOOME ESLE, RFO TA RWHETAVE TPNIO UYO EJUGD EHT RTOHE, UYO EAR GCNONIDMEN FYUOLESR, EBEACUS UYO OWH SPAS TJUNDEGM OD EHT EMSA STIHNG."

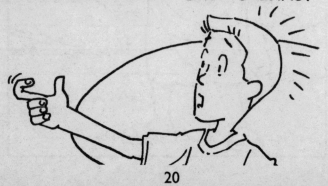

20

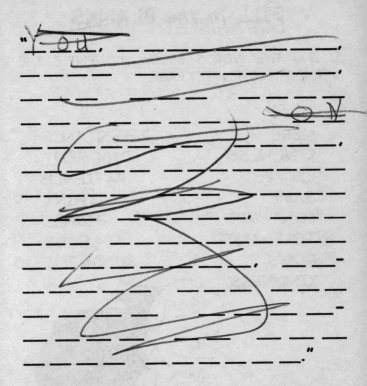

"Y o u , ___ ___ ___ ___ ,
___ ___ ___ ___ ___ ___ ,
___ ___ ___ ___ ___ ___ ___
___ ___ ___ ___ ___ ___ ___
___ ___ ___ ___ ___ ___ ,
___ ___ ___ ___ ___ ___ ___
___ ___ ___ ___ ___ ___ ___
___ ___ ___ ___ ___ ,
___ ___ ___ ___ ___ ___ -
___ ___ ___ ___ ___ ___ ___
___ ___ ___ ___ ___ , ___ -
___ ___ ___ ___ ___ ___ ___ -
___ ___ ___ ___ ___ ___ ___
___ ___ ___ ___ ___ ___ ."

ROMANS 2:1

FILL *in the* BLANKS

USING THE WORDS BELOW, COMPLETE THE VERSES ON THE NEXT PAGE.

MERE
KINDNESS
ESCAPE
SAME
CONTEMPT
TOLERANCE
GOD'S
KINDNESS

REPENTANCE
JUDGMENT
PATIENCE
THINK
RICHES
LEADS
JUDGMENT

FINISH THE VERSE

"SO WHEN YOU, A _____ MAN,
PASS _____ ON THEM
AND YET DO THE _____ THINGS,
DO YOU _____ YOU WILL
_____ GOD'S _____?
OR DO YOU SHOW _____
FOR THE _____ OF HIS
_____, _____
AND _____, NOT REALIZING
THAT _____ _____
_____ YOU TOWARD
_____?"

ROMANS 2:3-4

23

FINISH *the* VERSE

USE THE CODE CHART BELOW TO FINISH THE VERSES ON THE NEXT PAGE. (EXAMPLE: K=24)

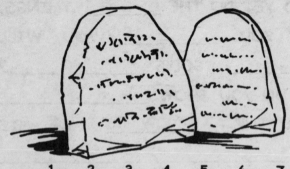

	1	2	3	4	5	6	7
1	A	B	C	D	E	F	G
2	H	I	J	K	L	M	N
3	O	P	Q	R	S	T	U
4	V	W	X	Y	Z		

"NOW ___ ___ ___, IF YOU CALL
    44 31 37

___ ___ ___ ___ ___ ___ ___ ___ A JEW;
44 31 37 34 35 15 25 16

IF YOU ___ ___ ___ ___ ON THE LAW
       34 15 25 44

AND ___ ___ ___ ___ ABOUT YOUR
    12 34 11 17

___ ___ ___ ___ ___ ___ ___ ___ ___ ___ ___ TO
34 15 25 11 36 22 31 27 35 21 22 32

___ ___ ___ ; IF YOU KNOW HIS ___ ___ ___ ___
17 31 14   42 22 25 25

AND ___ ___ ___ ___ ___ ___ ___ OF WHAT IS
    11 32 32 34 31 41 15

___ ___ ___ ___ ___ ___ ___ ___ BECAUSE YOU
35 37 32 15 34 22 31 34

ARE ___ ___ ___ ___ ___ ___ ___ ___ ___ ___ BY
    22 27 35 36 34 37 13 36 15 14

THE LAW."

ROMANS 2:17–18

25

DOUBLE *the* FUN

UNSCRAMBLE THE UNDERLINED WORDS IN EACH VERSE. ON THE NEXT PAGE, PLACE YOUR ANSWERS IN THE SPACES PROVIDED AND THEN COMPLETE THE CROSSWORD PUZZLE.

1. "IF YOU ARE <u>DCOENCVIN</u> THAT YOU ARE A GUIDE FOR THE <u>DBNLI</u>, A <u>TLHIG</u> FOR THOSE WHO ARE IN THE DARK."

ROMANS 2:19

2. "AN <u>RIOTNSTCRU</u> OF THE <u>LOFOSIH</u>, TEACHER OF INFANTS, BECAUSE YOU HAVE IN THE <u>WLA</u> THE EMBODIMENT OF KNOWLEDGE AND <u>TTHUR</u>."

ROMANS 2:20

3. "YOU, THEN, WHO <u>CHTAE</u> OTHERS, DO YOU NOT TEACH YOURSELF?"

ROMANS 2:21

1. _____ _____

_____

2. _____ _____

_____

3. _____

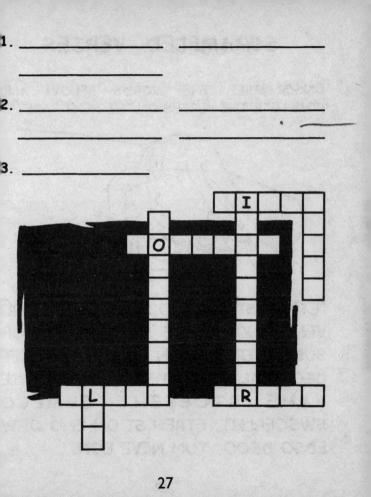

SCRAMBLED VERSES

UNSCRAMBLE THE WORDS BELOW AND COMPLETE THE VERSES ON THE NEXT PAGE.

"ETEHR SI ON ENO SRUIGOHET, TNO VENE ENO; ETHRE SI ON EON WOH SUDNDAERTNS, ON EON OHW SSKEE DGO. LAL EHVA DTEUNR YWAA, YHTE VAHE RTOEGEHT EBMECO SWSOERLHT; ETREH SI ON ENO OHW EDSO DGOO, TON NEVE EON."

"_____ ____ __ ___
___ _____,
___ ____ __ ___;
___ _____ _____ __ ___
___ __ _____ _____-
_____, __ __ ____
___ _____ _____ ___.
_____, _____ ___
_____ _____
_____; _____ __
__ ___ ____ ___
____ ___ ___ ___, ___
__ ___ ___ __ ___."

ROMANS 3:10–12

DOUBLE *the* FUN

UNSCRAMBLE THE UNDERLINED WORDS IN EACH VERSE. ON THE NEXT PAGE, PLACE YOUR ANSWERS IN THE SPACES PROVIDED AND THEN COMPLETE THE CROSSWORD PUZZLE.

1. "ALL HAVE <u>DTEUNR</u> AWAY, THEY HAVE TOGETHER BECOME <u>SWSOERLTH</u>;

ROMANS 3:12

2. "THERE IS NO <u>ENO</u> WHO DOES <u>DOGO</u>, NOT EVEN ONE."

ROMANS 3:12

3. "THEIR <u>TSTHARO</u> ARE OPEN GRAVES; THEIR TONGUES PRACTICE <u>TDIECE</u>. THE POISON OF <u>SVRIEP</u> IS ON THEIR <u>SLPI</u>."

ROMANS 3:13

1. _____ _____

2. _____ _____

3. _____ _____

   _____ _____

FINISH *the* VERSE

USE THE CODE CHART BELOW TO FINISH THE
VERSES ON THE NEXT PAGE. (EXAMPLE: K=24)

	1	2	3	4	5	6	7
1	A	B	C	D	E	F	G
2	H	I	J	K	L	M	N
3	O	P	Q	R	S	T	U
4	V	W	X	Y	Z		

32

"THEIR _ _ _ _ _ _ ARE
        26 31 37 36 21 35

FULL OF _ _ _ _ _ _ _
        13 37 34 35 22 27 17

AND BITTERNESS. THEIR FEET

ARE _ _ _ _ _ TO SHED
    35 42 22 16 36

_ _ _ _ _ ; RUIN AND
12 25 31 31 14

_ _ _ _ _ _ MARK THEIR
26 22 35 15 34 44

WAYS, AND THE WAY OF

_ _ _ _ _ THEY DO NOT
32 15 11 13 15

KNOW."

ROMANS 3:14–17

33

WORD SEARCH

FIND THE WORDS UNDERLINED BELOW IN THE WORD SEARCH ON THE NEXT PAGE.

"BUT NOW THE <u>RIGHTEOUSNESS</u> OF GOD WITHOUT THE <u>LAW</u> IS <u>MANIFESTED</u>, BEING WITNESSED BY THE LAW AND THE <u>PROPHETS</u>; EVEN THE RIGHTEOUSNESS OF <u>GOD</u> WHICH IS BY <u>FAITH</u> OF <u>JESUS</u> CHRIST UNTO ALL AND UPON ALL THEM THAT <u>BELIEVE</u>."

ROMANS 3:21–22, KJV

```
R R W B E L I E V E O B
F I Y D C E O U R E W L
T G G N P R O P H E T S
R H R E P R L G S R D K
K T C P Y E O X T R D N
H E Q O N T F U S E S B
F O G O B K E S T N T W
G U J V O L U S I L Y N
S S B E R B E L S A N T
P N T O U F D E B W I I
T E L H I B E J E S U S
R S T N I N D G O D N N
W S A T B S H I N B O V
H M P P B P T N Q S L N
Q F A I T H H N U H W V
```

35

SECRET CODES

TO SOLVE THE CODED VERSES BELOW, LOOK AT EACH LETTER AND WRITE THE ONE THAT COMES BEFORE IT IN THE ALPHABET.

"GPS BMM IBWF TJOOFE BOE GBMM TIPSU PG UIF HMPSZ PG HPE, BOE BSF KVTUJGJFE GSFFMZ CZ IJT HSBDF UISPVHI UIF SFEFNQUJPO UIBU DBNF CZ DISJTU KFTVT."

ABCDEFGHIJKLMNOPQRST
UVWXYZ

"FOR ALL HAVE
SINNED AND FALL
SHORT OF THE
_ _ _ _ _ _ _ _   _ _   _ _ _ ,
_ _ _   _ _ _ _ _ -
_ _ _ _ _ _ _   _ _ _ _ _
_ _   _ _   _ _ _ _
_ _ _ _ _ _ _ _   _ _ _ _
_ _ _ _ _ _ _ _ _   _ _ _ _
_ _ _   _ _   _ _ _ _ _ _
_ _ _ _ _ ."

ROMANS 3:23-24

37

CROSSWORD

ACROSS

1. "GOD PRESENTED HIM AS A SACRIFICE OF
   _____."
2. "THROUGH _____ IN HIS BLOOD."
3. "HE DID THIS TO DEMONSTRATE HIS
   _____."
4. "BECAUSE IN HIS FORBEARANCE HE HAD
   LEFT THE SINS _____ BEFOREHAND
   UNPUNISHED."

DOWN

1. "HE DID IT TO _____ HIS
   JUSTICE AT THE PRESENT TIME."
2. "SO AS TO BE _____."
3. "AND THE _____ WHO JUSTIFIES."
4. "THOSE WHO HAVE FAITH IN _____."

FILL *in the* BLANKS

USING THE WORDS BELOW, COMPLETE THE VERSES ON THE NEXT PAGE.

GENTILES
GOD
MAN
FAITH
LAW

JUSTIFIED
WORKS
DEEDS
BOASTING
JEWS

"WHERE IS _____ THEN? IT IS EXCLUDED. BY WHAT _____? OF _____? NAY: BUT BY THE LAW OF _____. THEREFORE WE CONCLUDE THAT A _____ IS _____ BY FAITH WITHOUT THE _____ OF THE LAW. IS HE THE _____ OF THE _____ ONLY? IS HE NOT ALSO OF THE GENTILES? YES, OF THE _____ ALSO."

ROMANS 3:27-29, KJV

COLOR *the* PICTURE

"SAYING, BLESSED ARE THEY WHOSE INIQUITIES ARE FORGIVEN, AND WHOSE SINS ARE COVERED. BLESSED IS THE MAN TO WHOM THE LORD WILL NOT IMPUTE SIN."

ROMANS 4:7–8, KJV

43

FINISH *the* VERSE

USE THE CODE CHART BELOW TO FINISH THE
VERSES ON THE NEXT PAGE. (EXAMPLE: K=24)

	1	2	3	4	5	6	7
1	A	B	C	D	E	F	G
2	H	I	J	K	L	M	N
3	O	P	Q	R	S	T	U
4	V	W	X	Y	Z		

"THEREFORE, SINCE WE HAVE BEEN __ __ __ __ __ __ __ __ __
23 37 35 36 22 16 22 15 14

THROUGH __ __ __ __ __ , WE
16 11 22 36 21

HAVE __ __ __ __ __ WITH GOD
32 15 11 13 15

THROUGH OUR __ __ __ __ JESUS
25 31 34 14

CHRIST, THROUGH WHOM WE HAVE GAINED ACCESS BY FAITH INTO THIS __ __ __ __ __ IN
17 34 11 13 15

WHICH WE NOW __ __ __ __ __."
35 36 11 27 14

ROMANS 5:1–2

45

SCRAMBLED VERSES

UNSCRAMBLE THE WORDS BELOW AND COMPLETE THE VERSES ON THE NEXT PAGE.

"TON YNLO OS, TUB EW OSLA ERECJOI NI URO SFUSFGENRI, EBSECUA EW WKON TAHT FUSFGENRI SPORUDEC EPCENRSAERVE; EPCENRSAERVE, CRHEATRCA; DAN TACARHCER, EPOH."

"_____ _____ _____,
_____ _____ _____
_____ _____ _____
_____ _____ _____,
_____ _____ _____
_____ _____ _____
_____ _____ _____;
_____ _____ _____,
_____ _____; _____
_____ _____ _____,
_____ _____"

ROMANS 5:3–4

47

WORD SEARCH

FIND THE WORDS UNDERLINED BELOW IN
THE WORD SEARCH ON THE NEXT PAGE.

"AND <u>HOPE</u> MAKETH NOT <u>ASHAMED</u>:

BECAUSE THE <u>LOVE</u> OF <u>GOD</u> IS SHED

<u>ABROAD</u> IN OUR <u>HEARTS</u> BY THE <u>HOLY</u>

<u>GHOST</u> WHICH IS <u>GIVEN</u> UNTO US."

ROMANS 5:5, KJV

```
V S H B E O B R S S I S
L H O P E R M P D H P T
W T Z O H U B I G O D Y
T R A T P B N D M S D D
E W A C T E S N S B F I
R H D P P B P D Z C H L
H O L Y V A B R O A D A
K S W I B B T T I N B S
F G Y D L O V E N P S H
T H O N C E I N T U H A
O O H E R S E D E K O M
K S C P D V D T L E U E
H T Q O I C L G E W L D
F S G G N T B X S R D D
G D J V H E A R T S T A
```

49

FILL *in the* BLANKS

USING THE WORDS BELOW, COMPLETE THE VERSES ON THE NEXT PAGE.

GOOD

RIGHTEOUS

POWERLESS

TIME

RARELY

DIED

JUST

UNGODLY

"YOU SEE, AT _____ THE RIGHT

_____, WHEN WE WERE STILL

_____, CHRIST _____

FOR THE _____. VERY

_____ WILL ANYONE DIE FOR

A _____ MAN, THOUGH

FOR A _____ MAN SOMEONE

MIGHT POSSIBLY DARE TO DIE."

ROMANS 5:6–7

SECRET CODES

TO SOLVE THE CODED VERSE BELOW, LOOK AT EACH LETTER AND WRITE THE ONE THAT COMES BEFORE IT IN THE ALPHABET.

"CVU HPE EFNPOTUSBUFT IJT   PXO MPWF GPS VT JO UIJT: XIJMF XF XFSF TUJMM TJOOFST, DISJTU EJFE GPS VT."

52

ABCDEFGHIJKLMNOPQRST
UVWXYZ

"_ _ _ _   _ _ _ _   _ _ _ _ _ _ -

_ _ _ _ _ _ _ _ _ _   _ _ _ _   _ _ _ _

_ _ _ _   _ _ _ _ _ _ _ _ _ _ _ _

_ _ _ _ _: _ _ _ _ _ _ _ _ _ _ _ _

_ _ _ _ _ _ _   _ _ _ _ _ _ _ _

_ _ _ _ _ _ _ _,   _ _ _ _ _ _ _

_ _ _ _ _ _ _ _   _ _ _ _   _ _."

ROMANS 5:8

FILL *in the* BLANKS

USING THE WORDS BELOW, COMPLETE THE
VERSES ON THE NEXT PAGE.

THROUGH   LIFE
DEATH   SAVED
RECONCILED   ENEMIES
HIM   WRATH
JUSTIFIED   BLOOD

"SINCE WE HAVE NOW BEEN

_____ BY HIS

_____, HOW MUCH MORE

SHALL WE BE _____ FROM

GOD'S _____ THROUGH

_____! FOR IF, WHEN WE WERE

GOD'S _____, WE WERE

_____ TO HIM

THROUGH THE _____ OF HIS

SON, HOW MUCH MORE, HAVING

BEEN RECONCILED, SHALL WE BE

SAVED _____ HIS _____!"

ROMANS 5:9–10

COLOR *the* PICTURE

"FOR IF, WHEN WE WERE ENEMIES, WE WERE RECONCILED TO GOD BY THE DEATH OF HIS SON, MUCH MORE, BEING RECONCILED, WE SHALL BE SAVED BY HIS LIFE."

ROMANS 5:10, KJV

FINISH *the* VERSE

USE THE CODE CHART BELOW TO FINISH THE
VERSES ON THE NEXT PAGE. (EXAMPLE: K=24)

	1	2	3	4	5	6	7
1	A	B	C	D	E	F	G
2	H	I	J	K	L	M	N
3	O	P	Q	R	S	T	U
4	V	W	X	Y	Z		

"THEREFORE, JUST AS __ __ __
35 22 27

ENTERED   THE   __ __ __ __ __
42 31 34 25 14

THROUGH   ONE   __ __ __,   AND
26 11 27

__ __ __ __ __   THROUGH   __ __ __,
14 15 11 36 21   35 22 27

AND IN THIS WAY DEATH CAME TO

__ __ __   MEN,   BECAUSE   ALL
11 25 25

__ __ __ __ __ __ —FOR BEFORE THE
35 22 27 27 15 14

__ __ __   WAS GIVEN, SIN WAS IN
25 11 42

THE __ __ __ __ __."
42 31 34 25 14

ROMANS 5:12–13

DOUBLE *the* FUN

UNSCRAMBLE THE UNDERLINED WORDS IN EACH VERSE. ON THE NEXT PAGE, PLACE YOUR ANSWERS IN THE SPACES PROVIDED AND THEN COMPLETE THE CROSSWORD PUZZLE.

1. "BUT THE GIFT IS NOT LIKE THE STSRAESP. FOR IF THE MANY IDED BY THE TRESPASS OF THE ONE MAN. . ."

ROMANS 5:15

2. "HOW MUCH MORE DID SGDO ECRAG AND THE GIFT THAT EMAC BY GRACE OF ONE MAN."

ROMANS 5:15

3. "JESUS SCTIRH, OWVOELFR TO THE MANY!"

ROMANS 5:15

1. _____ _____

2. _____ _____

_____

3. _____ _____

WORD SEARCH

FIND THE WORDS UNDERLINED BELOW IN THE WORD SEARCH ON THE NEXT PAGE.

"AGAIN, THE <u>GIFT</u> OF <u>GOD</u> IS NOT LIKE THE <u>RESULT</u> OF THE ONE MAN'S <u>SIN</u>: THE <u>JUDGMENT</u> FOLLOWED ONE SIN AND BROUGHT <u>CONDEMNATION</u>, BUT THE GIFT FOLLOWED MANY <u>TRESPASSES</u> AND BROUGHT <u>JUSTIFICATION</u>."

ROMANS 5:16

```
J U Y R I Y I U D E S C
U T C O J M V D T E E O
S O R D P D C L S E W N
T K K C O Y T S X S R D
I H R Q O N A F L T R E
F F J G V P L E D H P M
I G S J S O B O D S I N
C S D E O R G I L I T A
A P R T H U B D M S D T
T T P L F G I F T B F I
I R Z T T I S D Z C H O
O W R E S U L T K T K N
N H A P V B C T I N B N
J U D G M E N T B Q S O
K M W I B A I T T U C L
```

63

CROSSWORD

ACROSS

1. "FOR IF, BY THE _____ OF THE ONE MAN. . ."
2. "_____ REIGNED THROUGH THAT ONE MAN."
3. "HOW MUCH MORE WILL THOSE WHO _____."
4. "GOD'S ABUNDANT PROVISION OF _____."

DOWN

1. "AND OF THE GIFT OF _____."
2. "REIGN IN LIFE THROUGH THE ONE MAN, _____ CHRIST."
3. "CONSEQUENTLY, JUST AS THE RESULT OF ONE TRESPASS WAS CONDEMNATION FOR ALL _____."
4. "SO ALSO THE RESULT OF ONE _____ OF RIGHTEOUSNESS WAS JUSTIFICATION THAT BRINGS LIFE FOR ALL MEN."

FINISH *the* VERSE

USE THE CODE CHART BELOW TO FINISH THE
VERSE ON THE NEXT PAGE. (EXAMPLE: K=24)

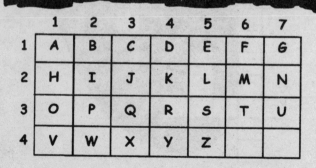

	1	2	3	4	5	6	7
1	A	B	C	D	E	F	G
2	H	I	J	K	L	M	N
3	O	P	Q	R	S	T	U
4	V	W	X	Y	Z		

"FOR JUST AS THROUGH THE

__ __ __ __ __ __ __ __ __ __ __
14 22 35 31 12 15 14 22 15 27 13 15

OF THE ONE MAN THE MANY WERE

MADE __ __ __ __ __ __ __ , SO
      35 22 27 27 15 34 35

ALSO   THROUGH   THE

__ __ __ __ __ __ __ __ __
31 12 15 14 22 15 27 13 15

OF   THE   ONE __ __ __ THE
                     26 11 27

__ __ __ __ WILL   BE   MADE
26 11 27 44

__ __ __ __ __ __ __ __ __ ."
34 22 17 21 36 15 31 37 35

ROMANS 5:19

SCRAMBLED VERSES

UNSCRAMBLE THE WORDS BELOW AND COMPLETE THE VERSES ON THE NEXT PAGE.

"TWHA LSLHA EW YSA, NTHE? LSLHA

EW OG NO GSNIINN OS TAHT EGARC

YMA EISNACER? YB ON SMNEA! EW

IDED OT NSI; WHO NCA EW ELVI NI

TI YNA RLEONG?"

"_____ _____ ___
____, _____? _____
__ __ __ _____
__ _____ __ __
___ _____?
__ ___ ___ __!
__ _____ _____;
____ ____ __ ___
__ ___ __ ___
_____?"

ROMANS 6:1-2

FILL in the BLANKS

USING THE WORDS BELOW, COMPLETE THE VERSES ON THE NEXT PAGE.

NEW
FATHER
GLORY
DEAD
JUST
CHRIST

BURIED
DEATH
BAPTIZED
ALL
LIFE
RAISED

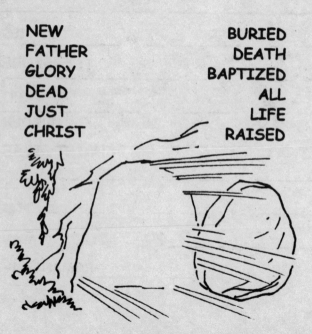

"OR DON'T YOU KNOW THAT
_____ OF US WHO WERE
_____ INTO _____
JESUS WERE BAPTIZED INTO HIS
_____? WE WERE THEREFORE
_____ WITH HIM THROUGH
BAPTISM INTO DEATH IN ORDER
THAT, _____ AS CHRIST WAS
_____ FROM THE _____
THROUGH THE _____ OF THE
_____, WE TOO MAY
LIVE A _____ _____."

ROMANS 6:3-4

DOUBLE *the* FUN

UNSCRAMBLE THE UNDERLINED WORDS IN EACH VERSE. ON THE NEXT PAGE, PLACE YOUR ANSWERS IN THE SPACES PROVIDED AND THEN COMPLETE THE CROSSWORD PUZZLE.

1. "IF WE HAVE BEEN <u>DUNETI</u> WITH HIM LIKE THIS IN HIS <u>HDTEA</u>, WE WILL CERTAINLY ALSO BE UNITED WITH <u>IMH</u> IN HIS RESURRECTION."

ROMANS 6:5

2. "FOR WE KNOW THAT OUR OLD SELF WAS <u>CDREUICFI</u> WITH HIM SO THAT THE BODY OF SIN <u>GTHMI</u> BE DONE AWAY WITH."

ROMANS 6:6

3. "THAT WE SHOULD NO LONGER BE SLAVES TO SIN—BECAUSE ANYONE WHO HAS <u>DDIE</u> HAS BEEN <u>EFERD</u> FROM SIN."

ROMANS 6:6–7

1. _____ _____

   _____ _____

2. _____ _____

3. _____ _____

FILL *in the* BLANKS

USING THE WORDS BELOW, COMPLETE THE VERSES ON THE NEXT PAGE.

DEATH
COUNT
CHRIST
DEAD
GOD

JESUS
YOURSELVES
SIN
ONCE
ALIVE

"THE _____ HE DIED, HE DIED TO SIN _____ FOR ALL; BUT THE LIFE HE LIVES, HE LIVES TO GOD. IN THE SAME WAY, _____ _____ _____ TO _____ BUT _____ TO _____ IN _____ _____."

ROMANS 6:10–11

SECRET CODES

TO SOLVE THE CODED VERSE BELOW, LOOK AT EACH LETTER AND WRITE THE ONE THAT COMES BEFORE IT IN THE ALPHABET.

"GPS TJO TIBMM OPU CF ZPVS

NBTUFS, CFDBVTF ZPV BSF OPU

VOEFS MBX, CVU VOEFS HSBDF."

A B C D E F G H I J K L M N O P Q R S T
U V W X Y Z

" _ _ _ _ _ _ _ _ _ _ _ _

_ _ _ _ _ _ _ _ _ _

_ _ _ _ _ _ , _ _ _ _ _ _ _ _

_ _ _ _ _ _ _ _ _ _ _

_ _ _ _ _ _ _ _ , _ _ _

_ _ _ _ _ _ _ _ _ _ . "

ROMANS 6:14

SCRAMBLED VERSES

UNSCRAMBLE THE WORDS BELOW AND COMPLETE THE VERSE ON THE NEXT PAGE.

"OS, YM SBRREOHT, UYO OASL DIDE OT HTE WLA THGHUOR ETH YBDO FO TCSHIR, THTA UYO TGMHI GBELNO OT RANEHTO, OT MIH OHW SWA DREASI MFRO HET DADE, NI DRROE HTTA EW TMGIH RBAE TFIUR OT DGO."

"_ _, _ _ _ _ _ _ _ _ _ _,

_ _ _ _ _ _ _ _ _ _ _ _ _ _

_ _ _ _ _ _ _ _ _ _ _ _ _

_ _ _ _ _ _ _ _ _ _ _ _

_ _ _ _ _ _ _ _, _ _ _ _ _ _ _ _

_ _ _ _ _ _ _ _ _ _ _ _ _

_ _ _ _ _ _ _, _ _ _ _ _

_ _ _ _ _ _ _ _ _ _ _ _ _

_ _ _ _ _ _ _ _ _ _ _ _ _,

_ _ _ _ _ _ _ _ _ _ _

_ _ _ _ _ _ _ _ _ _ _

_ _ _ _ _ _ _ _ _."

ROMANS 7:4

79

CROSSWORD

ROMANS 7:6, 7:21–22

ACROSS

1. "BUT NOW, BY DYING TO WHAT ONCE
   _____ US."
2. "WE HAVE BEEN RELEASED FROM THE _____."
3. "SO THAT WE SERVE IN THE NEW WAY OF
   THE _____."
4. "AND NOT IN THE _____ WAY OF THE
   WRITTEN CODE."

DOWN

1. "SO I FIND THIS LAW AT _____."
2. "WHEN I WANT TO DO _____."
3. "_____ IS RIGHT THERE WITH ME."
4. "FOR IN MY INNER BEING I _____
   IN GOD'S LAW."

WORD SEARCH

FIND THE WORDS UNDERLINED BELOW IN THE WORD SEARCH ON THE NEXT PAGE.

"THERE IS THEREFORE NOW NO <u>CONDEMNATION</u> TO <u>THEM</u> WHICH ARE IN <u>CHRIST</u> JESUS, WHO WALK NOT AFTER THE FLESH, BUT AFTER THE SPIRIT. FOR THE <u>LAW</u> OF THE <u>SPIRIT</u> OF <u>LIFE</u> IN CHRIST <u>JESUS</u> HATH MADE ME <u>FREE</u> FROM THE LAW OF <u>SIN</u> AND <u>DEATH</u>."

ROMANS 8:1–2, KJV

```
L M W I F R E E I Q S L
A B Y D B A Q N N U H W
W C T H E M E T T K O C
O T H E R T T D E E U O
K K C P S F R A E W L N
H R Q I Y C L G N R D D
F J R O N T B I S R T E
G H J V B K S L T I S M
C D B E O L E S S P T N
P E T O S P I R I T Y A
T P L H U M I L I D N T
R Z J E S U S M L F I I
W A C T I N E S I H L O
D E A T H S D Z F K N N
Q L R V B P H K E B O R
```

SECRET CODES

TO SOLVE THE CODED VERSE BELOW, LOOK
AT EACH LETTER AND WRITE THE ONE THAT
COMES BEFORE IT IN THE ALPHABET.

"GPS XIBU UIF MBX XBT QPXFSMFTT

UP EP JO UIBU JU XBT XFBLFOFE CZ

UIF TJOGVM OBUVSF, HPE EJE CZ

TFOEJOH IJT PXO TPO JO UIF

MJLFOFTT PG TJOGVM LBO UP CF B

TJO PGGFSJOH."

84

A B C D E F G H I J K L M N O P Q R S T
U V W X Y Z

"___ ___ ___
___ ___ _____-
___ ___ ___
___ ___ ___
___ ___ ___
___ ___ ___
___ ____, ___
___ __ ___
___ ___ ___
___ _____ ___
___ _____ ___
___ ___ ___ ___
_____ __."

ROMANS 8:3

85

FILL *in the* BLANKS

USING THE WORDS BELOW, COMPLETE THE VERSE ON THE NEXT PAGE.

SPIRIT

LAW

SINFUL

RIGHTEOUS

CONDEMNED

FULLY

LIVE

NATURE

"AND SO HE _____

SIN IN _____ MAN,   IN

ORDER THAT THE _____

REQUIREMENTS OF THE _____

MIGHT BE _____ MET IN US,

WHO DO NOT _____ACCORDING

TO THE SINFUL _____ BUT

ACCORDING TO THE _____."

ROMANS 8:3–4

FINISH *the* VERSE

USE THE CODE CHART BELOW TO FINISH THE
VERSE ON THE NEXT PAGE. (EXAMPLE: K=24)

	1	2	3	4	5	6	7
1	A	B	C	D	E	F	G
2	H	I	J	K	L	M	N
3	O	P	Q	R	S	T	U
4	V	W	X	Y	Z		

"THOSE WHO LIVE

$\overline{11}$ $\overline{13}$ $\overline{13}$ $\overline{31}$ $\overline{34}$ $\overline{14}$ $\overline{22}$ $\overline{27}$ $\overline{17}$

TO THE $\overline{35}$ $\overline{22}$ $\overline{27}$ $\overline{16}$ $\overline{37}$ $\overline{25}$

$\overline{27}$ $\overline{11}$ $\overline{36}$ $\overline{37}$ $\overline{34}$ $\overline{15}$ HAVE THEIR

$\overline{26}$ $\overline{22}$ $\overline{27}$ $\overline{14}$ $\overline{35}$ SET ON WHAT

THAT NATURE $\overline{14}$ $\overline{15}$ $\overline{35}$ $\overline{22}$ $\overline{34}$ $\overline{15}$ $\overline{35}$;

BUT THOSE WHO LIVE IN

ACCORDANCE WITH THE $\overline{35}$ $\overline{32}$ $\overline{22}$ $\overline{34}$ $\overline{22}$ $\overline{36}$

HAVE THEIR MINDS SET ON WHAT THE

SPIRIT $\overline{14}$ $\overline{15}$ $\overline{35}$ $\overline{22}$ $\overline{34}$ $\overline{15}$ $\overline{35}$."

ROMANS 8:5

89

COLOR *the* PICTURE

"FOR TO BE CARNALLY MINDED IS DEATH; BUT TO BE SPIRITUALLY MINDED IS LIFE AND PEACE. BECAUSE THE CARNAL MIND IS ENMITY AGAINST GOD: FOR IT IS NOT SUBJECT TO THE LAW OF GOD, NEITHER INDEED CAN BE."

ROMANS 8:6–7, KJV

SCRAMBLED VERSES

UNSCRAMBLE THE WORDS BELOW AND
COMPLETE THE VERSE ON THE NEXT PAGE.

"UYO, RHEOVWE, ERA DCEOLNLTOR

TON YB ETH LSUINF ENRAUT UBT YB

EHT TSIPRI, FI ETH TSIPRI FO DGO

SLEIV NI UYO."

"_ _ _, _ _ _ _ _ _ _,

_ _ _ _ _ _ _ _ _ _ _ _

_ _ _ _ _ _ _ _ _

_ _ _ _ _ _ _ _ _ _

_ _ _ _ _ _ _ _

_ _ _ _ _, _ _ _ _

_ _ _ _ _ _ _ _ _

_ _ _ _ _ _ _ _ _ _."

DOUBLE *the* FUN

UNSCRAMBLE THE UNDERLINED WORDS IN EACH VERSE. ON THE NEXT PAGE, PLACE YOUR ANSWERS IN THE SPACES PROVIDED AND THEN COMPLETE THE CROSSWORD PUZZLE.

1. "BUT IF <u>TCSHIR</u> IS IN YOU, YOUR BODY IS <u>DADE</u> BECAUSE OF SIN, YET YOUR <u>RSPITI</u> IS <u>EAVLI</u> BECAUSE OF RIGHTEOUSNESS."

ROMANS 8:10

2. "AND IF THE SPIRIT OF HIM WHO <u>DRAESI</u> JESUS FROM THE DEAD IS LIVING IN YOU, HE WHO RAISED CHRIST FROM THE DEAD WILL ALSO GIVE <u>IFEL</u> TO YOUR <u>LMAOTR</u> <u>SDIEOB</u> THROUGH HIS SPIRIT, WHO LIVES IN YOU."

ROMANS 8:11

1. _____   _____

_____   _____

2. _____   _____

_____   _____

FINISH *the* VERSE

USE THE CODE CHART BELOW TO FINISH THE
VERSE ON THE NEXT PAGE. (EXAMPLE: K=24)

	1	2	3	4	5	6	7
1	A	B	C	D	E	F	G
2	H	I	J	K	L	M	N
3	O	P	Q	R	S	T	U
4	V	W	X	Y	Z		

"FOR YOU DID NOT

_____ _____ _____ _____ _____ _____ _____ A
34   15   13   15   22   41   15

_____ _____ _____ _____ _____ _____ THAT MAKES
35   32   22   34   22   36

YOU A _____ _____ _____ _____ _____ AGAIN TO
        35   25   11   41   15

_____ _____ _____ _____, BUT YOU RECEIVED
16   15   11   34

THE _____ _____ _____ _____ _____ _____ OF
     35   32   22   34   22   36

_____ _____ _____ _____ _____ _____ _____. AND BY
35   31   27   35   21   22   32

HIM WE _____ _____ _____, '_____ _____ _____ _____,
       13   34   44   11   12   12   11

FATHER.'"

ROMANS 8:15

97

CROSSWORD

ROMANS 8:18–20

ACROSS

1. "I CONSIDER THAT OUR PRESENT _____."
2. "ARE NOT _____ COMPARING."
3. "_____ THE GLORY."
4. "THAT WILL BE REVEALED IN _____."

DOWN

1. "THE _____ WAITS IN EAGER EXPECTATION."
2. "FOR THE _____ OF GOD TO BE REVEALED."
3. "FOR THE CREATION WAS SUBJECTED TO _____."
4. "NOT BY ITS OWN _____, BUT BY THE WILL OF THE ONE WHO SUBJECTED IT."

99

SCRAMBLED VERSES

UNSCRAMBLE THE WORDS BELOW AND COMPLETE THE VERSE ON THE NEXT PAGE.

"EW NKWO ATHT ETH EWLHO

CNROAITE SHA NBEE RGNAONIG SA

NI EHT NSPIA FO DCHLIHBTRI TRHIG

PU OT EHT TPNRESE EITM."

"_____ _____ _____ _____ _____

_____ _____ _____ _____

_____ _____ _____ _____

_____ _____ _____

____ ___ _____ _____

____ _____ _____ _____

_____ _____ ___ ___ ___

_____ _____ ___ ___ ___."

ROMANS 8:22

SECRET CODES

TO SOLVE THE CODED VERSE BELOW, LOOK AT EACH LETTER AND WRITE THE ONE THAT COMES BEFORE IT IN THE ALPHABET.

"OPU POMZ TP, CVU XF PVSTFMWFT,

XIP IBWF UIF GJSTUGSVJUT PG UIF

TQJSJU, HSPBO JOXBSEMZ BT XF

XBJU FBHFSMZ GPS PVS BEPQUJPO

BT TPOT, UIF SFEFNQUJPO PG PVS

CPEJFT."

A B C D E F G H I J K L M N O P Q R S T
U V W X Y Z

"___ ___ ___   ___ ___ ___ ___   ___ ___,

___ ___ ___ ___   ___ ___   ___ ___ ___ ___ -

___ ___ ___ ___ ___ ___ ___,   ___ ___ ___ ___

___ ___ ___ ___ ___   ___ ___ ___ ___ ___ ___ -

___ ___ ___ ___ ___ ___   ___ ___   ___ ___ ___ ___

___ ___ ___ ___ ___,   ___ ___ ___ ___

___ ___ ___ ___ ___ ___ ___ ___   ___ ___   ___ ___ ___ -

___ ___ ___ ___   ___ ___ ___   ___ ___ ___ ___

___ ___ ___ ___   ___ ___ ___   ___ ___ ___ ___ -

___ ___ ___ ___   ___ ___ ___   ___ ___ ___ ___,

___ ___ ___ ___   ___ ___ ___ ___   ___ ___ ___ ___ -

___ ___ ___ ___   ___ ___   ___ ___ ___ ___

___ ___ ___ ___ ___ ___ ___ ___."

ROMANS 8:23

103

FILL *in the* BLANKS

USING THE WORDS BELOW, COMPLETE THE VERSES ON THE NEXT PAGE.

HOPE   PATIENTLY
SAVED   HE
SEEN   WHAT
NO   HAVE

"FOR IN THIS _____ WE WERE

_____. BUT HOPE THAT IS

_____ IS _____ HOPE AT ALL.

WHO HOPES FOR WHAT _____

ALREADY HAS? BUT IF WE HOPE FOR

_____ WE DO NOT YET

_____, WE WAIT FOR IT

_____."

ROMANS 8:24-25

DOUBLE *the* FUN

UNSCRAMBLE THE UNDERLINED WORDS IN EACH VERSE. ON THE NEXT PAGE, PLACE YOUR ANSWERS IN THE SPACES PROVIDED AND THEN COMPLETE THE CROSSWORD PUZZLE.

1. "IN THE SAME WAY, THE SPIRIT HELPS US IN OUR SWESAENK."

ROMANS 8:26

2. "WE DO NOT KNOW WHAT WE OUGHT TO YPAR FOR, BUT THE SPIRIT FHLIEMS INTERCEDES FOR US WITH SGNRAO THAT SWDOR CANNOT EXPRESS."

ROMANS 8:26

3. "AND HE WHO SSEAEHRC OUR HEARTS KNOWS THE MIND OF THE TSIRIP, BECAUSE THE SPIRIT SIENDTEECR FOR THE SAINTS IN ACCORDANCE WITH GOD'S WILL."

ROMANS 8:27

1. _____

2. _____   _____

   _____   _____

3. _____   _____

   _____

WORD SEARCH

FIND THE WORDS UNDERLINED BELOW IN THE WORD SEARCH ON THE NEXT PAGE.

"AND HE THAT <u>SEARCHETH</u> THE <u>HEARTS</u> KNOWETH WHAT IS THE MIND OF THE <u>SPIRIT</u>, BECAUSE HE MAKETH <u>INTERCESSION</u> FOR THE <u>SAINTS</u> <u>ACCORDING</u> TO THE <u>WILL</u> OF GOD."

ROMANS 8:27, KJV

```
H E A R T S S B X S R D
T G S J V T K F L T R T
G S D B N O T E S S I S
D P E I O I B V D H N E
O T A L R U M I L I T A
R S Z I F B B D M E E R
F W P C T I N E G B R C
K S A P P B S N Z C C H
L Q L R V B I H K T E E
K M W I B D C T I N S T
V N T Y R C E W E S S H
T C O O C E I T T U I W
O T C E R H K B R Z O B
K C C P D V D T R E N L
A R Q O Y C L W I L L R
```

SCRAMBLED VERSES

UNSCRAMBLE THE WORDS BELOW AND COMPLETE THE VERSE ON THE NEXT PAGE.

"DNA EW WNKO THTA NI LAL STGHNI DGO SKRWO RFO EHT DGOO FO ETHSO OWH ELVO MHI, OHW EVHA NEBE DCAELL GANCICDOR OT SHI EPSUORP."

"___ ___ ___   ___ ___   ___ ___ ___

___ ___ ___ ___   ___ ___ ___   ___ ___ ___

___ ___ ___ ___   ___   ___ ___ ___

___ ___ ___ ___   ___ ___ ___ ___   ___ ___ ___

___ ___ ___   ___ ___   ___ ___ ___

___ ___ ___ ___   ___ ___ ___ ___   ___ ___ ___,

___ ___ ___   ___ ___ ___ ___   ___ ___

___ ___ ___ ___ ___ ___   ___ ___ ___ ___ ___ ___-

___ ___ ___   ___ ___ ___   ___ ___ ___ ___

___ ___ ___ ___ ___ ___ ___."

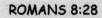

ROMANS 8:28

FILL *in the* BLANKS

USING THE WORDS BELOW, COMPLETE THE VERSE ON THE NEXT PAGE.

BROTHERS	CONFORMED
FIRSTBORN	PREDESTINED
SON	GOD
LIKENESS	FOREKNEW

"FOR THOSE _____

_____ HE ALSO

_____ TO BE

_____ TO THE

_____ OF HIS _____,

THAT HE MIGHT BE THE

_____ AMONG MANY

_____."

ROMANS 8:29

DOUBLE *the* FUN

UNSCRAMBLE THE UNDERLINED WORDS IN EACH VERSE. ON THE NEXT PAGE, PLACE YOUR ANSWERS IN THE SPACES PROVIDED AND THEN COMPLETE THE CROSSWORD PUZZLE.

1. "AND THOSE HE DPREDENESIT, HE ALSO CALLED; THOSE HE CALLED, HE ALSO DJEUSITFI; THOSE HE JUSTIFIED, HE ALSO GDELOIRIF."

ROMANS 8:30

2. "WHAT, THEN, LALSH WE SAY IN RESPONSE TO ISHT?"

ROMANS 8:31

3. "IF DGO IS FOR US, WHO CAN BE ATGSANI US?"

ROMANS 8:31

1. _____ _____

_____

2. _____ _____

3. _____ _____

FINISH *the* VERSE

USE THE CODE CHART BELOW TO FINISH THE
VERSE ON THE NEXT PAGE. (EXAMPLE: K=24)

	1	2	3	4	5	6	7
1	A	B	C	D	E	F	G
2	H	I	J	K	L	M	N
3	O	P	Q	R	S	T	U
4	V	W	X	Y	Z		

"HE WHO DID ___ ___ ___
27 31 36

___ ___ ___ ___ ___   HIS OWN
35 32 11 34 15

___ ___ ___,   BUT GAVE   ___ ___ ___
35 31 27   21 22 26

UP FOR US   ___ ___ ___ — HOW
            11 25 25

WILL HE NOT   ___ ___ ___ ___,
              11 25 35 31

ALONG   WITH   ___ ___ ___,
               21 22 26

___ ___ ___ ___ ___ ___ ___ ___ ___ ___
17 34 11 13 22 31 37 35 25 44

GIVE US ALL ___ ___ ___ ___ ___ ___?"
            36 21 22 27 17 35

ROMANS 8:32

117

FILL *in the* BLANKS

USING THE WORDS BELOW, COMPLETE THE VERSES ON THE NEXT PAGE.

CREATION
DEATH
SEPARATE
ANGELS
POWERS
CONVINCED

GOD
LIFE
LOVE
PRESENT
HEIGHT
DEMONS

"FOR I AM _____ THAT

NEITHER _____ NOR _____,

NEITHER _____ NOR

_____, NEITHER THE

_____ NOR THE FUTURE, NOR

ANY _____, NEITHER _____

NOR DEPTH, NOR ANYTHING ELSE IN

ALL _____, WILL BE ABLE TO

_____ US FROM THE

_____ OF _____ THAT IS IN

CHRIST JESUS OUR LORD."

ROMANS 8:38–39

119

SECRET CODES

TO SOLVE THE CODED VERSE BELOW, LOOK AT EACH LETTER AND WRITE THE ONE THAT COMES BEFORE IT IN THE ALPHABET.

"XIBU UIFO TIBMM XF TBZ? UIBU UIF

HFOUJMFT, XIP EJE OPU QVSTVF

SJHIUFPVTOFTT, IBWF PCUBJOFE JU,

B SJHIUFPVTOFTT UIBU JT CZ

GBJUI."

"_____ _____ _____

__ ___? _____ ____

_____, __ __ _

____ ____ ____

_____,

____ ____ ____

__, _ _____ _-

____ ____ __ __

_____."

ROMANS 9:30

CROSSWORD

ROMANS 9:31–33

ACROSS

1. "BUT ISRAEL, WHO PURSUED A LAW OF RIGHTEOUSNESS, HAS NOT _____ IT."
2. "WHY NOT? BECAUSE THEY _____ IT NOT BY FAITH."
3. "BUT AS IF IT WERE BY _____."
4. "THEY _____ OVER THE 'STUMBLING STONE.'"

DOWN

1. "AS IT IS WRITTEN: 'SEE, I LAY IN ZION A _____.'"
2. "'THAT CAUSES _____ TO STUMBLE.'"
3. "'AND A ROCK THAT MAKES THEM _____.'"
4. "'AND THE ONE WHO _____ IN HIM WILL NEVER BE PUT TO SHAME.'"

SCRAMBLED VERSES

UNSCRAMBLE THE WORDS BELOW AND COMPLETE THE VERSE ON THE NEXT PAGE.

"SBRORETH, YM SHTRAE EDERIS DAN RPARYE OT DGO RFO ETH ISSERATIEL SI TAHT YTHE YAM EB DSVAE."

"＿＿＿＿＿＿＿＿,　＿＿

＿＿＿＿＿　＿＿＿＿＿

＿＿＿＿　＿＿＿＿＿

＿＿＿　＿＿＿　＿＿

＿＿＿＿＿＿＿

＿＿　＿＿＿＿　＿＿＿

＿＿＿　＿＿＿　＿＿＿＿＿."

ROMANS 10:1

FINISH *the* VERSE

USE THE CODE CHART BELOW TO FINISH THE
VERSE ON THE NEXT PAGE. (EXAMPLE: K=24)

	1	2	3	4	5	6	7
1	A	B	C	D	E	F	G
2	H	I	J	K	L	M	N
3	O	P	Q	R	S	T	U
4	V	W	X	Y	Z		

"FOR I CAN T E S T I F Y
$\underline{T}$ $\underline{E}$ $\underline{S}$ $\underline{T}$ $\underline{I}$ $\underline{F}$ $\underline{Y}$
36 15 35 36 22 16 44

ABOUT T H E M THAT THEY
$\underline{T}$ $\underline{H}$ $\underline{E}$ $\underline{M}$
36 21 15 26

ARE ___ ___ ___ ___ ___ ___ ___ FOR
45 15 11 25 31 37 35

___ ___ ___, BUT THEIR ___ ___ ___ ___
17 31 14   45 15 11 25

IS NOT BASED ON ___ ___ ___ ___ -
24 27 31 42

___ ___ ___ ___ ___."
25 15 14 17 15

ROMANS 10:2

127

WORD SEARCH

FIND THE WORDS LISTED BELOW IN THE WORD SEARCH ON THE NEXT PAGE.

COMES

GODS

SOUGHT

ESTABLISH

KNOW

GOD

RIGHTEOUSNES

SUBMIT

```
E S T C E P A Q N S N R
G O N M J E B V S M Q I
E U K R P S U B M I T G
H G R Q L Y V D M F G H
K H J G O N C L G P F T
Y T S J G O D S X B F E
R A D B E B D F H X A O
F P N T P E L S S C T U
M G O D R B I C X U F S
L R Z T E L V D H V S N
J W A C B R B D M D S E
F H A A P I K N O W E S
Z Q T R V B J D Z B N S
X S W I B B P E K C I D
E B Y D N B C O M E S Q
```

COLOR *the* PICTURE

"'SEE, I LAY IN ZION A STONE THAT CAUSES MEN TO STUMBLE AND A ROCK THAT MAKES THEM FALL, AND THE ONE WHO TRUSTS IN HIM WILL NEVER BE PUT TO SHAME.'"

ROMANS 9:33

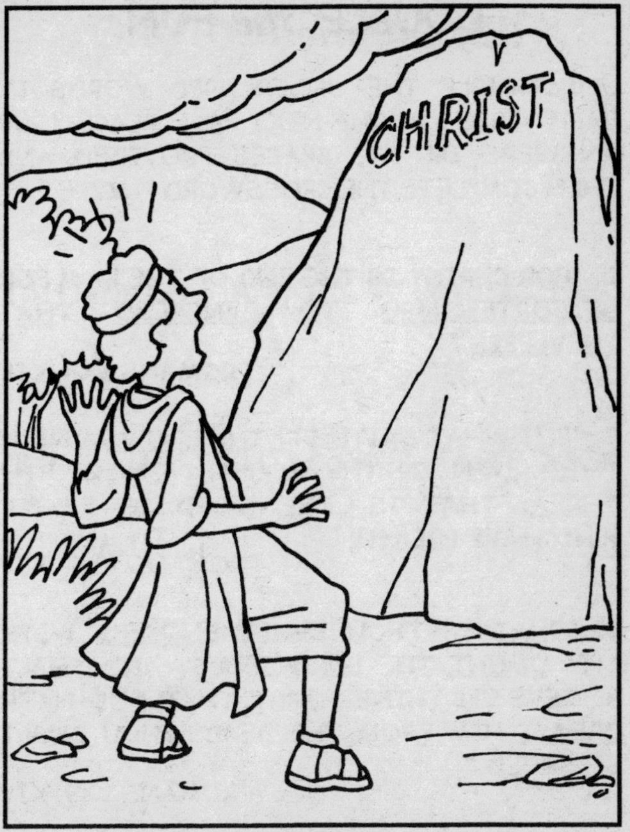
CHRIST

DOUBLE *the* FUN

UNSCRAMBLE THE UNDERLINED WORDS IN EACH VERSE. ON THE NEXT PAGE, PLACE YOUR ANSWERS IN THE SPACES PROVIDED AND THEN COMPLETE THE CROSSWORD PUZZLE.

1. "FOR CHRIST IS THE END OF THE LAW FOR <u>SEIGORTEHSNSU</u> TO <u>EVNEREYO</u> THAT <u>THEVLEBIE</u>."

ROMANS 10:4, KJV

2. "BUT WHAT SAITH IT? THE <u>DROW</u> IS NIGH THEE, EVEN IN THY MOUTH, AND IN THY <u>THREA</u>: THAT IS, THE WORD OF FAITH, WHICH WE PREACH."

ROMANS 10:8, KJV

3. "THAT IF THOU SHALT <u>SNOCEFS</u> WITH THY <u>OMUHT</u> THE LORD JESUS, AND SHALT BELIEVE IN THINE HEART THAT GOD HATH <u>DREASI</u> HIM FROM THE DEAD, THOU SHALT BE SAVED."

ROMANS 10:9, KJV

1. _____ _____

_____

2. _____ _____

3. _____ _____

_____

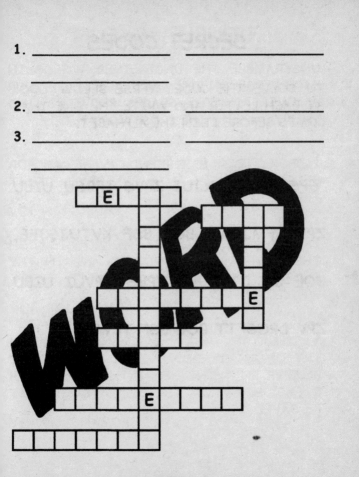

SECRET CODES

TO SOLVE THE CODED VERSE BELOW, LOOK
AT EACH LETTER AND WRITE THE ONE THAT
COMES BEFORE IT IN THE ALPHABET.

"GPS JU JT XJUI ZPVS IFBSU UIBU

ZPV CFMJFWF BOE BSF KVTUJGJFE,

BOE JU JT XJUI ZPVS NPVUI UIBU

ZPV DPOGFTT BOE BSF TBWFE."

ABCDEFGHIJKLMNOPQRST
UVWXYZ

"___ ___ ___ ___ ___

___ ___ ___ ___ ___

___ ___ ___ ___ ___

___ _____,'

___ ___ ___ ___

___ ___ ___ ___

___ ___ ___

___ ___ _____."

ROMANS 10:10

FILL *in the* BLANKS

USING THE WORDS BELOW, COMPLETE THE VERSES ON THE NEXT PAGE.

TRUSTS	SHAME
SAVED	DIFFERENCE
NAME	GENTILE
CALLS	LORD
BLESSES	SCRIPTURE

"AS THE _____ SAYS,
'ANYONE WHO _____ IN HIM
WILL NEVER BE PUT TO _____.'
FOR THERE IS NO _____
BETWEEN JEW AND _____—THE
SAME _____ IS LORD OF ALL AND
RICHLY _____ ALL WHO
CALL ON HIM, FOR, 'EVERYONE WHO
_____ ON THE _____ OF THE
LORD WILL BE _____.'"

ROMANS 10:11–13

137

SCRAMBLED VERSES

UNSCRAMBLE THE WORDS BELOW AND COMPLETE THE VERSE ON THE NEXT PAGE.

"I KAS HTNE: IDD DGO JERTEC SHI EPEPOL? YB ON SNMAE! I MA NA SIARLETIE YMESFL, A EDCSNEADTN FO BAARAHM, MFOR EHT RTBIE FO EBJNMANI."

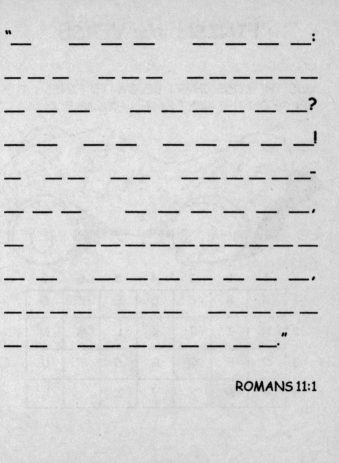

"_ ___ _ ___ __:

___ ___ ___ ___

_ __ _ _____?

__ __ _ _____!

_ __ __ _____-

___ ___ _____,

_ _____

__ __ _____,

____ ___ ____

__ _____."

ROMANS 11:1

FINISH *the* VERSE

USE THE CODE CHART BELOW TO FINISH THE
VERSE ON THE NEXT PAGE. (EXAMPLE: K=24)

	1	2	3	4	5	6	7
1	A	B	C	D	E	F	G
2	H	I	J	K	L	M	N
3	O	P	Q	R	S	T	U
4	V	W	X	Y	Z		

"_ _ _ DID NOT _ _ _ _ _ _
17 31 14   34 15 23 15 13 36

HIS _ _ _ _ _ _, WHOM HE
    32 15 31 32 25 15

_ _ _ _ _ _ _ _. DON'T YOU KNOW
16 31 34 15 24 27 15 42

WHAT THE _ _ _ _ _ _ _ _ _
       35 13 34 22 32 36 37 34 15

SAYS IN THE _ _ _ _ _ _ _
             32 11 35 35 11 17 15

ABOUT _ _ _ _ _ _ – HOW HE
     15 25 22 23 11 21

_ _ _ _ _ _ _ _ TO _ _ _
11 32 32 15 11 25 15 14   17 31 14

AGAINST ISRAEL."

ROMANS 11:2

141

CROSSWORD

ROMANS 11:3–5

ACROSS

1. "LORD, THEY HAVE KILLED YOUR _____.'"
2. "'AND TORN DOWN YOUR _____.'"
3. "'I AM THE ONLY ONE _____.'"
4. "'AND THEY ARE TRYING TO KILL _____.'"

DOWN

1. "AND WHAT WAS GOD'S _____ TO HIM?"
2. "'I HAVE _____ FOR MYSELF.'"
3. "'SEVEN THOUSAND WHO HAVE NOT BOWED THE _____ TO BAAL.'"
4. "SO TOO, AT THE PRESENT _____ THERE IS A REMNANT CHOSEN BY GRACE."

WORD SEARCH

FIND THE WORDS UNDERLINED BELOW IN THE WORD SEARCH ON THE NEXT PAGE.

"EVEN SO THEN AT THIS <u>PRESENT</u> <u>TIME</u> ALSO THERE IS A <u>REMNANT</u> ACCORDING TO THE <u>ELECTION</u> OF GRACE. AND IF BY GRACE, THEN IS IT NO <u>MORE</u> OF <u>WORKS</u>: <u>OTHERWISE</u> GRACE IS NO MORE <u>GRACE</u>."

ROMANS 11:5–6, KJV

```
K M W I B B C T I N B O
F B Y D B A Q N N Q S L
T C H E L E C T I O N W
O T H E R S T D E K O B
K M O R E E R T T E U L
H R Q O Y C L N E W L R
F J G O N T E Z S R D D
G S J V B S F L T R T A
S D B E E L E S S E S G
P E T R R S V D H M T R
T P P H K M I L I N Y A
R Z T R B B D M S A N C
W A O T I M E S B N I E
H W P P B S D Z C T L O
Q W O T H E R W I S E N
```

145

SCRAMBLED VERSES

UNSCRAMBLE THE WORDS BELOW AND COMPLETE THE VERSE ON THE NEXT PAGE.

"HTREFEORE, I RUEG UOY, RBTOEHSR,

NI IVEW FO DGOS YMREC, OT FOFRE

OURY   OBDEIS   SA   ILIVGN

ASRCFICISE, OHYL NAD LPAESNIG OT

DGO—HTSI SI RYUO ISPIRUTLA CAT

FO OWRHSPI."

"__ ___ ___ ___ ___ ___ ___,
__ ___ ___ ___ ___ ___,
__ ___ ___ ___ ___, __
___ ___ __ ___
_____, ___ ___
___ ___ ___ ___
__ ____ ____-
____, ___ ___
_____ __ ___
____ __ ____
_____ ___
__ _____."

ROMANS 12:1

FILL *in the* BLANKS

USING THE WORDS BELOW, COMPLETE THE
VERSE ON THE NEXT PAGE.

CONFORM
PLEASING
APPROVE
TEST
MIND

PATTERN
WORLD
TRANSFORMED
RENEWING
WILL

"DO NOT _____ ANY

LONGER TO THE _____ OF

THIS _____, BUT BE

_____ BY THE

_____ OF YOUR _____.

THEN YOU WILL BE ABLE TO

_____ AND _____

WHAT GOD'S WILL IS—HIS GOOD,

_____ AND PERFECT

_____."

ROMANS 12:2

149

CROSSWORD

ROMANS 12:9–11

ACROSS

1. "LOVE MUST BE _____."
2. "HATE WHAT IS _____."
3. "_____ TO WHAT IS GOOD."
4. "BE DEVOTED TO _____ ANOTHER."

DOWN

1. "IN _____ LOVE."
2. "HONOR ONE _____ ABOVE
   YOURSELVES."
3. "_____ BE LACKING IN ZEAL."
4. "BUT KEEP YOUR _____ FERVOR,
   SERVING THE LORD."

SECRET CODES

TO SOLVE THE CODED VERSES BELOW, LOOK AT EACH LETTER AND WRITE THE ONE THAT COMES BEFORE IT IN THE ALPHABET.

"CMFTT UIPTF XIP QFSTFDVUF ZPV;

CMFTT BOE EP OPU DVSTF. SFKPJDF

XJUI UIPTF XIP SFKPJDF; NPVSO

XJUI UIPTF XIP NPVSO."

152

ABCDEFGHIJKLMNOPQRST
UVWXYZ

"_____ _____ ___

_____ ___;

_____ ___ ___

_____. _____

____ _____ ___

_____; _____

____ ___ ___

_____."

ROMANS 12:14–15

FINISH *the* VERSE

USE THE CODE CHART BELOW TO FINISH THE
VERSE ON THE NEXT PAGE. (EXAMPLE: K=24)

	1	2	3	4	5	6	7
1	A	B	C	D	E	F	G
2	H	I	J	K	L	M	N
3	O	P	Q	R	S	T	U
4	V	W	X	Y	Z		

"ON THE __ __ __ __ __ __ __ __ :
13 31 27 36 34 11 34 44

IF YOUR __ __ __ __ __ IS
15 27 15 26 44

__ __ __ __ __ __ , __ __ __ __
21 37 27 17 34 44   16 15 15 14

HIM; IF HE IS __ __ __ __ __ __ __ ,
36 21 22 34 35 36 44

GIVE __ __ __ SOMETHING TO
21 22 26

__ __ __ __ __ . IN __ __ __ __ __
14 34 22 27 24   14 31 22 27 17

THIS, YOU __ __ __ __ __ __ __ __
42 22 25 25   21 15 11 32

__ __ __ __ __ __ __ __ __ __ __
12 37 34 27 22 27 17   13 31 11 25 35

ON HIS __ __ __ __ ."
21 15 11 14

ROMANS 12:20

155

DOUBLE *the* FUN

UNSCRAMBLE THE UNDERLINED WORDS IN EACH VERSE. ON THE NEXT PAGE, PLACE YOUR ANSWERS IN THE SPACES PROVIDED AND THEN COMPLETE THE CROSSWORD PUZZLE.

"<u>VENOREYE</u> MUST <u>TSIUMB</u> <u>FLIMESH</u> TO THE <u>OGINGREVN</u> AUTHORITIES, FOR THERE IS NO AUTHORITY <u>TEPCXE</u> THAT WHICH GOD HAS <u>EDEHSILBATS</u>. THE <u>SEITIROHTUA</u> THAT EXIST HAVE <u>NEBE</u> ESTABLISHED BY <u>ODG</u>."

ROMANS 13:1

FINISH *the* VERSE

USE THE CODE CHART BELOW TO FINISH THI
VERSE ON THE NEXT PAGE. (EXAMPLE: K=24)

	1	2	3	4	5	6	7
1	A	B	C	D	E	F	G
2	H	I	J	K	L	M	N
3	O	P	Q	R	S	T	U
4	V	W	X	Y	Z		

159

FINISH *the* VERSE

USE THE CODE CHART BELOW TO FINISH THE
VERSE ON THE NEXT PAGE. (EXAMPLE: K=24)

	1	2	3	4	5	6	7
1	A	B	C	D	E	F	G
2	H	I	J	K	L	M	N
3	O	P	Q	R	S	T	U
4	V	W	X	Y	Z		

"ACCEPT ___ ___ ___ WHOSE
        21 22 26

___ ___ ___ ___ ___ IS ___ ___ ___ ___,
16 11 22 36 21   42 15 11 24

WITHOUT ___ ___ ___ ___ ___ ___ ___
        32 11 35 35 22 27 17

___ ___ ___ ___ ___ ___ ___ ___
23 37 14 17 26 15 27 36

ON ___ ___ ___ ___ ___ ___ ___ ___ ___ ___
   14 22 35 32 37 36 11 12 25 15

MATTERS."

ROMANS 14:1

161

FILL *in the* BLANKS

USING THE WORDS BELOW, COMPLETE THE VERSE ON THE NEXT PAGE.

PLEASE   STRONG
BUILD   BEAR
SHOULD   FAILINGS
GOOD   WEAK
NEIGHBOR   OURSELVES

"WE WHO ARE _____ OUGHT

TO _____ WITH THE

_____ OF THE

_____ AND NOT TO PLEASE

_____. EACH OF US

_____ _____ HIS

_____ FOR HIS

_____, TO _____ HIM UP."

ROMANS 15:1–2

SECRET CODES

TO SOLVE THE CODED VERSE BELOW, LOOK AT EACH LETTER AND WRITE THE ONE THAT COMES BEFORE IT IN THE ALPHABET.

"GPS FWFO DISJTU EJE OPU QMFBTF

IJNTFMG CVU, BT JU JT XSJUUFO:

'UIF JOTVMUT PG UIPTF XIP JOTVMU

ZPV IBWF GBMMFO PO NF.'"

A B C D E F G H I J K L M N O P Q R S T
U V W X Y Z

"___ ___ ___ ___

___ ___ ___ ___

___ ___ ___ ___ ___ ___ ,

___ ___ ___ ___ _____:

___ ___ ___ ___ ___

___ ___ ___ ___ ___

___ ___ ___ ___ ___

___ ___ ___.'"

ROMANS 15:3

165

FILL *in the* BLANKS

USING THE WORDS BELOW, COMPLETE THE VERSE ON THE NEXT PAGE.

SPIRIT   FILL
POWER   PEACE
HOPE   OVERFLOW
TRUST   GOD
JOY   HOLY
YOU   HIM

"MAY THE _____ OF HOPE

_____ YOU WITH ALL _____

AND _____ AS YOU

_____ IN _____, SO

THAT _____ MAY _____

WITH _____ BY THE

_____ OF THE _____

_____."

ROMANS 15:13

COLOR *the* PICTURE

"WE THEN THAT ARE STRONG OUGHT TO BEAR THE INFIRMITIES OF THE WEAK, AND NOT TO PLEASE OURSELVES. LET EVERY ONE OF US PLEASE HIS NEIGHBOUR FOR HIS GOOD TO EDIFICATION. FOR EVEN CHRIST PLEASED NOT HIMSELF; BUT, AS IT IS WRITTEN, THE REPROACHES OF THEM THAT REPROACHED THEE FELL ON ME."

ROMANS 15:1–3, KJV

169

1. <u>GOSPEL</u>   <u>PROPHETS</u>
2. <u>SPIRIT</u>   <u>POWER</u>
3. <u>GRACE</u>   <u>FATHER</u>

<u>CHRIST</u>

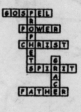

PG. 9

PG. 11

"I AM NOT <u>ASHAMED</u> OF THE <u>GOSPEL</u> BECAUSE IT IS THE <u>POWER</u> OF <u>GOD</u> FOR THE <u>SALVATION</u> OF <u>EVERYONE</u> WHO BELIEVES: FIRST FOR THE <u>JEW</u>, THEN FOR THE <u>GENTILE</u>."

ROMANS 1:16

"<u>THE WRATH OF GOD IS BEING REVEALED FROM HEAVEN AGAINST ALL THE GODLESSNESS AND WICKEDNESS OF MEN WHO SUPPRESS THE TRUTH BY THEIR WICKEDNESS, SINCE WHAT MAY BE KNOWN ABOUT GOD IS PLAIN TO THEM, BECAUSE GOD HAS MADE IT PLAIN TO THEM.</u>"

ROMANS 1:18-19

```
H R Q L F A T H E R F D
F J G O N C L M F K C W
G S J V P O W E R A A B
R D S E B D F E R R K L
A N P P E L W G G O R R
C P I R B W O R K S O D
E Z R E B V C X U R S T
W A I T R B C H R I S T
H A T P I N T M E J E W
Q L R V C T S S D C L
M W I R E R D P E A C E
B Y D F C E K C H L Q
T C R P A G E N T I L E
N E J E B G E N T E N W
P R O P H E T S Q I O P
```

"FOR SINCE THE __CREATION__ OF THE __WORLD__ GOD'S __INVISIBLE__ QUALITIES— HIS __ETERNAL__ POWER AND __DIVINE__ NATURE—HAVE BEEN __CLEARLY__ SEEN, BEING __UNDERSTOOD__ FROM WHAT HAS BEEN __MADE__, SO THAT __MEN__ ARE WITHOUT __EXCUSE__."

ROMANS 1:20

Crossword answers:
- GLORY
- GLORIFIED
- B
- CAME
- ANIMALS
- FUTILE
- CLAIMED
- HEARTS
- GOD

"YOU, THEREFORE HAVE NO EXCUSE, YOU WHO PASS JUDGMENT ON SOMEONE ELSE, FOR AT WHATEVER POINT YOU JUDGE THE OTHER, YOU ARE CONDEMNING YOURSELF, BECAUSE YOU WHO PASS JUDGMENT DO THE SAME THINGS."

ROMANS 2:1

"SO WHEN YOU, A __MERE__ MAN, PASS __JUDGMENT__ ON THEM AND YET DO THE __SAME__ THINGS, DO YOU __THINK__ YOU WILL __ESCAPE__ GOD'S __JUDGMENT__ ? OR DO YOU SHOW __CONTEMPT__ FOR THE __RICHES__ OF HIS __KINDNESS__, TOLERANCE AND __PATIENCE__, NOT REALIZING THAT __GOD'S__ __KINDNESS__ __LEADS__ YOU TOWARD __REPENTANCE__ ?"

ROMANS 2:3-4

"NOW __YOU__, IF YOU CALL __YOURSELF__ A JEW: IF YOU __RELY__ ON THE LAW AND __BRAG__ ABOUT YOUR __RELATIONSHIP__ TO __GOD__: IF YOU KNOW HIS __WILL__ AND __APPROVE__ OF WHAT IS __SUPERIOR__ BECAUSE YOU ARE __INSTRUCTED__ BY THE LAW."

ROMANS 2:17-18

1. CONVINCED   BLIND
   LIGHT
2. INSTRUCTOR   LAW
   TRUTH   FOOLISH
3. TEACH

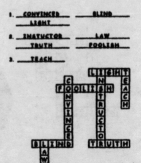

172

"THERE IS NO ONE RIGHTEOUS NOT EVEN ONE; THERE IS NO ONE WHO UNDER-STANDS, NO ONE WHO SEEKS GOD. ALL HAVE TURNED AWAY, THEY HAVE TOGETHER BECOME WORTHLESS; THERE IS NO ONE WHO DOES GOOD, NOT EVEN ONE."

ROMANS 3:10-12

1. TURNED   WORTHLESS
2. ONE   GOOD
3. THROATS   DECEIT
   VIPERS   LIPS

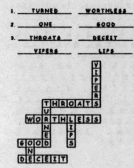

"THEIR M O U T H S ARE FULL OF C U R S I N G AND BITTERNESS. THEIR FEET ARE S W I F T TO SHED B L O O D; RUIN AND M I S E R Y MARK THEIR WAYS, AND THE WAY OF P E A C E THEY DO NOT KNOW."

ROMANS 3:14-17

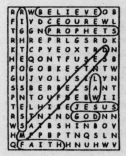

ABCDEFGHIJKLMNOPQRST
UVWXYZ

"FOR ALL HAVE SINNED AND FALL SHORT OF THE GLORY OF GOD, AND ARE JUSTIFIED FREELY BY HIS GRACE THROUGH THE REDEMPTION THAT CAME BY CHRIST JESUS."

ROMANS 3:23–24

Crossword:

- JESUS (down)
- JUSTICE (across)
- DEMONSTRATE (down)
- JUST (down)
- ATONEMENT (across)
- COMMITTED (across)
- FAITH (across)

"WHERE IS _BOASTING_ THEN? IT IS EXCLUDED. BY WHAT _LAW_? OF _WORKS_? NAY: BUT BY THE LAW OF _FAITH_. THEREFORE WE CONCLUDE THAT A _MAN_ IS _JUSTIFIED_ BY FAITH WITHOUT THE _DEEDS_ OF THE LAW. IS HE THE _GOD_ OF THE _JEWS_ ONLY? IS HE NOT ALSO OF THE GENTILES? YES, OF THE _GENTILES_ ALSO."

ROMANS 3:27–29, KJV

"THEREFORE, SINCE WE HAVE BEEN J U S T I F I E D THROUGH F A I T H, WE HAVE P E A C E WITH GOD THROUGH OUR L O R D JESUS CHRIST, THROUGH WHOM WE HAVE GAINED ACCESS BY FAITH INTO THIS G R A C E IN WHICH WE NOW S T A N D."

ROMANS 5:1-2

"N O T O N L Y S O, B U T W E A L S O R E J O I C E I N O U R S U F F E R I N G S, B E C A U S E W E K N O W T H A T S U F F E R I N G P R O D U C E S P E R S E V E R A N C E; P E R S E V E R A N C E, C H A R A C T E R; A N D C H A R A C T E R, H O P E."

ROMANS 5:3-4

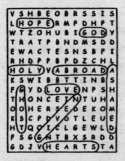

"YOU SEE, AT JUST THE RIGHT TIME, WHEN WE WERE STILL POWERLESS, CHRIST DIED FOR THE UNGODLY. VERY RARELY WILL ANYONE DIE FOR A RIGHTEOUS MAN, THOUGH FOR A GOOD MAN SOMEONE MIGHT POSSIBLY DARE TO DIE."

ROMANS 5:6-7

ABCDEFGHIJKLMNOPQRST
UVWXYZ

"BUT GOD DEMON-
STRATES HIS OWN
LOVE FOR US IN
THIS: WHILE WE
WERE STILL
SINNERS, CHRIST
DIED FOR US."

ROMANS 5:8

"SINCE WE HAVE NOW BEEN
JUSTIFIED BY HIS
BLOOD , HOW MUCH MORE
SHALL WE BE SAVED FROM
GOD'S WRATH THROUGH
HIM ! FOR IF, WHEN WE WERE
GOD'S ENEMIES , WE WERE
RECONCILED TO HIM
THROUGH THE DEATH OF HIS
SON, HOW MUCH MORE, HAVING
BEEN RECONCILED, SHALL WE BE
SAVED THROUGH HIS LIFE !"

ROMANS 5:9-10

"THEREFORE, JUST AS S I N
ENTERED THE W O R L D
THROUGH ONE M A N, AND
D E A T H THROUGH S I N,
AND IN THIS WAY DEATH CAME TO
A L L MEN, BECAUSE ALL
S I N N E D —FOR BEFORE THE
L A W WAS GIVEN, SIN WAS IN
THE W O R L D."

ROMANS 5:12-13

176

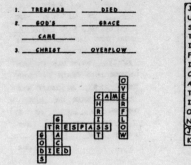

1. TRESPASS — DIED
2. GOD'S — GRACE
   CAME
3. CHRIST — OVERFLOW

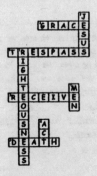

"FOR JUST AS THROUGH THE

__D I S O B E D I E N C E__

OF THE ONE MAN THE MANY WERE

MADE __S I N N E R S__. SO

ALSO THROUGH THE

__O B E D I E N C E__

OF THE ONE __M A N__ THE

__M A N Y__ WILL BE MADE

__R I G H T E O U S__."

ROMANS 5:19

"WHAT SHALL WE SAY, THEN? SHALL WE GO ON SINNING SO THAT GRACE MAY INCREASE? BY NO MEANS! WE DIED TO SIN; HOW CAN WE LIVE IN IT ANY LONGER?

ROMANS 6:1-2

"OR DON'T YOU KNOW THAT __ALL__ OF US WHO WERE __BAPTIZED__ INTO __CHRIST__ JESUS WERE BAPTIZED INTO HIS __DEATH__ ? WE WERE THEREFORE __BURIED__ WITH HIM THROUGH BAPTISM INTO DEATH IN ORDER THAT, __JUST__ AS CHRIST WAS __RAISED__ FROM THE __DEAD__ THROUGH THE __GLORY__ OF THE __FATHER__. WE TOO MAY LIVE A __NEW__ __LIFE__."

ROMANS 6:3-4

1. __UNITED__   __DEATH__
   __HIM__
2. __CRUCIFIED__   __MIGHT__
3. __DIED__   __FREED__

"THE __DEATH__ HE DIED, HE DIED TO SIN __ONCE__ FOR ALL; BUT THE LIFE HE LIVES, HE __LIVES__ TO GOD. IN THE SAME WAY, __COUNT__ __YOURSELVES__ __DEAD__ TO __SIN__ BUT __ALIVE__ TO __GOD__ IN __CHRIST__ __JESUS__."

ROMANS 6:10-11

178

ABCDEFGHIJKLMNOPQRST
UVWXYZ

"FOR SIN SHALL
NOT BE YOUR
MASTER, BECAUSE
YOU ARE NOT
UNDER LAW, BUT
UNDER GRACE."

ROMANS 6:14

"SO, MY BROTHERS,
YOU ALSO DIED TO
THE LAW THROUGH
THE BODY OF
CHRIST, THAT YOU
MIGHT BELONG TO
ANOTHER, TO HIM
WHO WAS RAISED
FROM THE DEAD,
IN ORDER THAT
WE MIGHT BEAR
FRUIT TO GOD."

ROMANS 7:4

ABCDEFGHIJKLMNOPQRST
UVWXYZ

"FOR WHAT THE
LAW WAS POWER-
LESS TO DO IN
THAT IT WAS
WEAKENED BY
THE SINFUL
NATURE. GOD
DID BY SENDING
HIS OWN SON IN
THE LIKENESS
OF SINFUL MAN
TO BE A SIN
OFFERING."

ROMANS 8:3

"AND SO HE **CONDEMNED**
SIN IN **SINFUL** MAN, IN
ORDER THAT THE **RIGHTEOUS**
REQUIREMENTS OF THE **LAW**
MIGHT BE **FULLY** MET IN US,
WHO DO NOT **LIVE** ACCORDING
TO THE SINFUL **NATURE** BUT
ACCORDING TO THE **SPIRIT**."

ROMANS 8:3-4

"THOSE WHO LIVE
A C C O R D I N G
TO THE S I N F U L
N A T U R E HAVE THEIR
M I N D S SET ON WHAT
THAT NATURE D E S I R E S;
BUT THOSE WHO LIVE IN
ACCORDANCE WITH THE S P I R I T
HAVE THEIR MINDS SET ON WHAT THE
SPIRIT D E S I R E S."

ROMANS 8:5

"YOU, HOWEVER,
ARE CONTROLLED
NOT BY THE
SINFUL NATURE
BUT BY THE
SPIRIT, IF THE
SPIRIT OF GOD
LIVES IN YOU."

ROMANS 8:9

1. ___CHRIST___   ___DEAD___
   ___SPIRIT___   ___ALIVE___
2. ___RAISED___   ___LIFE___
   ___MORTAL___   ___BODIES___

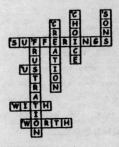

"FOR YOU DID NOT
R E C E I V E A
S P I R I T THAT MAKES
YOU A S L A V E AGAIN TO
F E A R, BUT YOU RECEIVED
THE S P I R I T OF
S O N S H I P, AND BY
HIM WE C R Y, 'A B B A,
FATHER.'"

ROMANS 8:15

"WE KNOW THAT THE WHOLE CREATION HAS BEEN GROANING AS IN THE PAINS OF CHILDBIRTH RIGHT UP TO THE PRESENT TIME."

ROMANS 8:22

ABCDEFGHIJKLMNOPQRST
UVWXYZ

"NOT ONLY SO BUT WE OUR-SELVES, WHO HAVE THE FIRST-FRUITS OF THE SPIRIT GROAN INWARDLY AS WE WAIT EAGERLY FOR OUR ADOP-TION AS SONS, THE REDEMP-TION OF OUR BODIES."

ROMANS 8:23

"FOR IN THIS _HOPE_ WE WERE _SAVED_. BUT HOPE THAT IS _SEEN_ IS _NO_ HOPE AT ALL. WHO HOPES FOR WHAT _HE_ ALREADY HAS? BUT IF WE HOPE FOR _WHAT_ WE DO NOT YET _HAVE_, WE WAIT FOR IT _PATIENTLY_."

ROMANS 8:24-25

1. _WEAKNESS_
2. _PRAY_   _HIMSELF_
   GROANS   _WORDS_
3. _SEARCHES_ _SPIRIT_
   INTERCEDES

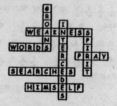

```
H E A R T S S B X S R D
T G S J V Y K F L T R T
G S D N O T E S S I S
D P E I I B V D H N E
O T A R D M I L I T S
R S T I F B B D M E E
F W P C T I N E G B R
K S A P P S N C C C H
L Q L R V P I A K T E
K M W I R D C T I N S T
V N T Y R C E W E S H
T C O C E I T T U I W
O T C E R H K B R Z O
K C P D V D T R E N L
A R Q O Y C L W I L L R
```

"AND WE KNOW THAT IN ALL THINGS GOD WORKS FOR THE GOOD OF THOSE WHO LOVE HIM, WHO HAVE BEEN CALLED ACCORDING TO HIS PURPOSE."

ROMANS 8:28

"FOR THOSE ___GOD___ ___FOREKNEW___ HE ALSO ___PREDESTINED___ TO BE ___CONFORMED___ TO THE ___LIKENESS___ OF HIS ___SON___. THAT HE MIGHT BE THE ___FIRSTBORN___ AMONG MANY ___BROTHERS___."

ROMANS 8:29

1. ___PREDESTINED___ ___JUSTIFIED___ ___GLORIFIED___
2. ___SHALL___ ___THIS___
3. ___GOD___ ___AGAINST___

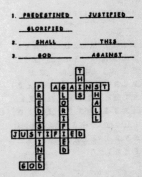

183

"HE WHO DID __N__ __O__ __T__
__S__ __P__ __A__ __R__ __E__ HIS OWN
__S__ __O__ __N__, BUT GAVE __H__ __I__ __M__
UP FOR US __A__ __L__ __L__—HOW
WILL HE NOT __A__ __L__ __S__ __O__,
ALONG WITH __H__ __I__ __M__,
__G__ __R__ __A__ __C__ __I__ __O__ __U__ __S__ __L__ __Y__
GIVE US ALL __T__ __H__ __I__ __N__ __G__ __S__?"

ROMANS 8:32

"FOR I AM __CONVINCED__ THAT
NEITHER __DEATH__ NOR __LIFE__,
NEITHER __ANGELS__ NOR
__DEMONS__ NEITHER THE
__PRESENT__ NOR THE FUTURE, NOR
ANY __POWERS__, NEITHER __HEIGHT__
NOR DEPTH, NOR ANYTHING ELSE IN
ALL __CREATION__ WILL BE ABLE TO
__SEPARATE__ US FROM THE
__LOVE__ OF __GOD__ THAT IS IN
CHRIST JESUS OUR LORD."

ROMANS 8:38-39

ABCDEFGHIJKLMNOPQRST
UVWXYZ

__WHAT__ __THEN__ __SHALL__
__WE__ __SAY__? __THAT__ __THE__
__GENTILES__, __WHO__
__DID__ __NOT__ __PURSUE__
__RIGHTEOUSNESS__,
__HAVE__ __OBTAINED__
__IT__, __A__ __RIGHTEOUS-__
__NESS__ __THAT__ __IS__ __BY__
__FAITH__."

ROMANS 9:30

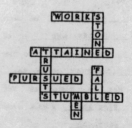

184

"BROTHERS, MY
HEART'S DESIRE
AND PRAYER TO
GOD FOR THE
ISRAELITES
IS THAT THEY
MAY BE SAVED."

ROMANS 10:1

"FOR I CAN T E S T I F Y

ABOUT T H E M THAT THEY

ARE Z E A L O U S FOR

G O D, BUT THEIR Z E A L

IS NOT BASED ON K N O W-

L E D G E."

ROMANS 10:2

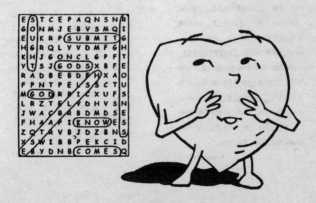

185

1. RIGHTEOUSNESS   EVERYONE
   BELIEVETH
2.   WORD   HEART
3.   CONFESS   MOUTH
   RAISED

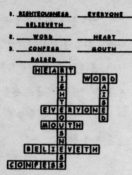

ABCDEFGHIJKLMNOPQRST
UVWXYZ

"FOR IT IS WITH
YOUR HEART THAT
YOU BELIEVE AND
ARE JUSTIFIED,
AND IT IS WITH
YOUR MOUTH THAT
YOU CONFESS
AND ARE SAVED."

ROMANS 10:10

"AS THE ___SCRIPTURE___ SAYS,
'ANYONE WHO ___TRUSTS___ IN HIM
WILL NEVER BE PUT TO ___SHAME___.'
FOR THERE IS NO ___DIFFERENCE___
BETWEEN JEW AND ___GENTILE___ — THE
SAME ___LORD___ IS LORD OF ALL AND
RICHLY ___BLESSES___ ALL WHO
CALL ON HIM. FOR, 'EVERYONE WHO
___CALLS___ ON THE ___NAME___ OF THE
LORD WILL BE ___SAVED___.'"

ROMANS 10:11-13

"I ASK THEN:
DID GOD REJECT
HIS PEOPLE?
BY NO MEANS!
I AM AN ISRAEL-
ITE MYSELF,
A DESCENDANT
OF ABRAHAM,
FROM THE TRIBE
OF BENJAMIN."

ROMANS 11:1

PG. 141

"**G O D** DID NOT **R E J E C T**
13 14   19 13 23 13 25 20

HIS **P E O P L E,** WHOM HE
24 19 24 24 29 19

F O R E K N E W. DON'T YOU KNOW
14 14 18 19 14 25 19 40

WHAT THE **S C R I P T U R E**
26 13 24 11 24 20 34 34 19

SAYS IN THE **P A S S A G E**
24 11 26 26 11 15 19

ABOUT **E L I J A H** – HOW HE
19 20 11 21 11 14

A P P E A L E D TO **G O D**
11 24 24 19 11 20 19 10   13 14 14

AGAINST ISRAEL."

ROMANS 11:2

PG. 143

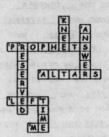

PG. 145

```
K M W I B B C T I N B O
F B Y D B A Q N N Q S L
T C H E L E C T I O N W
O T H E R S T D E K O B
K M O R E E R T T E U L
H R Q O Y C I N E W L R
F J G O N T E E S R D D
G S J V B S E L T R T A
S D B E E L E S S E S G
P E T R O S V D H M T R
T P P A K M I L I N Y A
R Z T R B B D M S A N C
W A O T I M E S B N I E
H W F P B S D Z C T L O
Q W O T H E R W I S E N
```

PG. 147

"**T H E R E F O R E,
I U R G E Y O U,
B R O T H E R S, I N
V I E W O F G O D'S
M E R C Y, T O O F F E R
Y O U R B O D I E S
A S L I V I N G S A C R I-
F I C E S, H O L Y A N D
P L E A S I N G T O G O D
– T H I S I S Y O U R
S P I R I T U A L A C T
O F W O R S H I P.**"

ROMANS 12:1

"DO NOT __CONFORM__ ANY
LONGER TO THE __PATTERN__ OF
THIS __WORLD__. BUT BE
__TRANSFORMED__ BY THE
__RENEWING__ OF YOUR __MIND__.
THEN YOU WILL BE ABLE TO
__TEST__ AND __APPROVE__
WHAT GOD'S WILL IS—HIS GOOD,
__PLEASING__ AND PERFECT
__WILL__."

ROMANS 12:2

ABCDEFGHIJKLMNOPQRST
UVWXYZ

"BLESS THOSE WHO
PERSECUTE YOU;
BLESS AND DO NOT
CURSE. REJOICE
WITH THOSE WHO
REJOICE; MOURN
WITH THOSE WHO
MOURN."

ROMANS 12:14-15

"ON THE __CONTRARY__,
IF YOUR __ENEMY__ IS
__HUNGRY__, FEED
HIM; IF HE IS __THIRSTY__,
GIVE __HIM__ SOMETHING TO
__DRINK__ IN __DOING__
THIS, YOU __WILL__ __HEAP__
__BURNING__ __COALS__
ON HIS __HEAD__."

ROMANS 12:20

EVERYONE · SUBMIT · HIMSELF · GOVERNING · EXCEPT · ESTABLISHED · AUTHORITIES · BEEN · GOD

"ACCEPT **H I M** WHOSE
F A I T H IS **W E A K**
WITHOUT **P A S S I N G**
J U D G E M E N T
ON **D I S P U T A B L E**
MATTERS."

ROMANS 14:1

"WE WHO ARE **STRONG** OUGHT
TO **BEAR** WITH THE
FAILINGS OF THE
WEAK AND NOT TO PLEASE
OURSELVES. EACH OF US
SHOULD **PLEASE** HIS
NEIGHBOR FOR HIS
GOOD, TO **BUILD** HIM UP."

ROMANS 15:1-2

ABCDEFGHIJKLMNOPQRST
UVWXYZ

"FOR EVEN CHRIST
DID NOT PLEASE
HIMSELF BUT,
AS IT IS WRITTEN:
THE INSULTS OF
THOSE WHO INSULT
YOU HAVE FALLEN
ON ME:"

ROMANS 15:3

"MAY THE _GOD_ OF HOPE
FILL YOU WITH ALL _JOY_
AND _PEACE_ AS YOU
TRUST IN _HIM_, SO
THAT _YOU_ MAY _OVERFLOW_
WITH _HOPE_ BY THE
POWER OF THE _HOLY_
SPIRIT."

ROMANS 15:13

SUPER BIBLE ACTIVITIES FOR KIDS!

Barbour's Super Bible Activity Books, packed with fun illustrations and kid-friendly text, will appeal to children ages six to twelve. And the price—only $1.39—will appeal to parents. All books are paperbound. The unique size (4⅛" x 5⅜") makes these books easy to take anywhere!

A Great Selection to Satisfy All Kids!

Bible Activities
Bible Activities for Kids
Bible Connect the Dots
Bible Crosswords for Kids
Bible Picture Fun
Bible Word Games
Bible Word Searches for Kids
Clean Jokes for Kids
Fun Bible Trivia

Fun Bible Trivia 2
Great Bible Trivia for Kids
More Bible Activities
More Bible Crosswords for Kids
More Clean Jokes for Kids
Super Bible Activities
Super Bible Crosswords
Super Bible Word Searches
Super Silly Stories

Available wherever books are sold.
Or order from: Barbour Publishing, Inc.
P.O. Box 719
Uhrichsville, Ohio 44683
www.barbourbooks.com

If ordering by mail,
please include $1.00 for postage and handling per order.
Prices subject to change without notice.